After those we love the most

Just have no way of knowing

The many things the heart conceals...

Presented to

Ashley Barrett

from

Jenna Froberg

Books in the Just Because Series
Moments of Celebration
Moments of Comfort
Moments of Friendship
Moments of Love

Other beloved books by Helen Steiner Rice
A New Beginning
An Instrument of Your Peace
An Old-Time Christmas
Blossoms of Friendship
Celebrations of the Heart
For Each New Day
Gifts of Love
God's Promises from A to Z
Inspiration for Living
Loving Promises
Lovingly: Poems for All Seasons
Mother, I Love You
Somebody Loves You
Someone Cares
To Mother with Love

THE
Just Because
SERIES

Moments of Friendship

HELEN STEINER RICE

Fleming H. Revell
A Division of Baker Book House Co
Grand Rapids, Michigan 49516

© 2002 by Virginia Ruehlmann
and The Helen Steiner Rice Foundation

Published by Fleming H. Revell
a division of Baker Book House Company
P.O. Box 6287, Grand Rapids, MI 49516-6287

Poems taken from *Blossoms of Friendship* by Helen Steiner Rice, compiled
by Virginia Ruehlmann, published in 1992. Biographical information
drawn from *Helen Steiner Rice: Ambassador of Sunshine* by Ronald Pollitt
and Virginia Wiltse, published in 1994.

Printed in the United States of America

Library of Congress Cataloging-in-Publication Data is on file at the
Library of Congress, Washington, D.C.

ISBN 0-8007-1801-1

Photo on cover and page 1 © Johner/Photonica
Photo on pages 46–47 © Jake Rajs/Photonica

Cover and interior design by Robin Black

For current information about all releases from Baker Book House, visit
our web site:
                    http://www.bakerbooks.com

Friendship,
Moment by Moment

The Nature of Friendship

Like the dear ones themselves, the poems, photos, notes, and letters of Helen Steiner Rice show how the bond between friends endures all things. There Helen is on her twenty-first birthday in May of 1921—her shiny hair swept into a loose chignon and her arms struggling to encircle all the birthday bouquets of flowers from suitors, coworkers, and friends. Then, in her thirties, Helen leans a bobbed head against the pillar of the cruise ship that she and lifelong friend Dorothy Gradison took across the Great Lakes to Canada.

In her forties, Helen beams across a table for three in the restaurant she frequented. Letters received in her fifties and sixties, even to the end of her life at 81, bear the same names, and photos show the same faces. Helen believed that friends are forever, whether they are with you or not.

Look at the scrapbook of your life, be it in a treasure chest or somewhere in your memory. Who are the comrades? Where are the kind and kindred spirits? What are the affinities and what is this affection that you share?

Life is a garden,
    good friends are the flowers,
And time spent together,
    life's happiest hours;
And friendship, like flowers,
    blooms ever more fair
When carefully tended
    by dear friends who care;
And life's lovely garden
    would be sweeter by far
If all who passed through it
    were as nice as you are.

Friendship is a priceless gift
    that cannot be bought or sold,
But its value is far greater
    than a mountain made of gold.
For gold is cold and lifeless,
    it can neither see nor hear,
And in the time of trouble
    it is powerless to cheer.
It has no ears to listen,
    no heart to understand,
It cannot bring you comfort,
    or reach out a helping hand.
So when you ask God for a gift,
    be thankful if He sends
Not diamonds, pearls, or riches,
    but the love of real true friends.

People need people and friends need friends,
And we all need love for a full life depends
Not on vast riches or great acclaim,
Not on success or on worldly fame
But just knowing that someone cares
And holds us close in thoughts and prayers.
For only the knowledge that we're understood
Makes everyday living feel wonderfully good.
And we rob ourselves of life's greatest need
When we lock up our hearts and fail to heed
The outstretched hand reaching to find
A kindred spirit whose heart and mind
Are lonely and longing to somehow share
Our joys and sorrows to make us aware
That life's completeness and richness depends
On the things we share with loved ones and friends.

Friendship is a golden chain,
The links are friends so dear,
And like a rare and precious jewel
It's treasured more each year.
It's clasped together firmly
With a love that's deep and true,
And it's rich with happy memories
And fond recollections, too.
Time can't destroy its beauty
For, as long as memory lives,
Years can't erase the pleasure
That the joy of friendship gives.
For friendship is a priceless gift
That can't be bought or sold,
And to have an understanding friend
Is worth far more than gold,
And the golden chain of friendship
Is a strong and blessed tie
Binding kindred hearts together
As the years go passing by.

Life is like a garden

And friendship like a flower
That blooms and grows in beauty
With the sunshine and the shower.

And lovely are the blossoms
That are tended with great care
By those who work unselfishly
To make the place more fair.

And in the garden of the heart
Friendship's flower opens wide
When we shower it with kindness
As our love shines from inside.

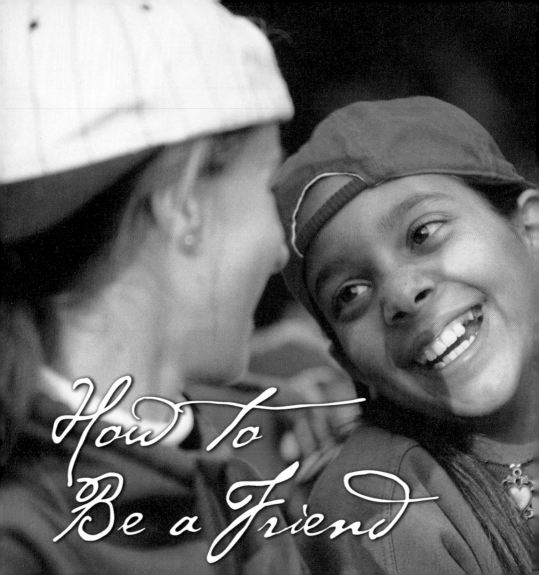

*How to
Be a Friend*

Helen's yearly, original-verse Christmas cards became famous, but she showed her friends how she valued them with more than this once-a-year token. After being invited to the wedding of friends, she continued to commemorate the occasion with original anniversary poems and letters for the next forty-five years. When she learned a coworker had been mugged walking to his nearby home from the office one evening, she started working late so they could make the daily trek together.

She gave one of her dearest friends a gold coin left to her by her beloved husband, Franklin, who had vowed to commemorate with a new coin every month of their marriage. Of course, the Great Depression struck, and tragedy followed with Franklin's suicide. And then Helen learned deeper lessons of friendship. In addition to the fun and fondness, the recipe calls for prayer, compassion, and unselfish care. And there were other lessons, evident in her verse and poetry.

Often during a busy day
I pause for a minute
to silently pray.
I mention the names
of those I love
And treasured friends
I am fondest of.
For it doesn't matter
where we pray
If we honestly mean
the words that we say,
For God is always
listening to hear
The prayers that are made
by a heart that's sincere.

An unlit candle gives no light,
Only when it's burning is it shining bright.
And life is empty, dull, and dark,
Until doing things for others gives the needed spark
That sets a useless life on fire
And fills the heart with new desire.

In this troubled world
    it's refreshing to find
Someone who still has
    the time to be kind,
Someone who still has
    the faith to believe
That the more you give
    the more you receive,
Someone who's ready
    by thought, word, or deed
To reach out a hand
    in the hour of need.

New Friends

Helen believed the world was full of friends—folks she simply hadn't met yet. Her actions showed this more than anything. Where many people might not take the time to get to know the person who rings up the groceries most weeks at the supermarket, or the two or three regular clerks at the post office, Helen did.

Her maid at the Gibson Hotel, where she lived most of her life, became so loving a friend that Helen teasingly called her "Mom." Later in life, her drivers to and from work at Gibson Art Company became personal friends who were mentioned in her letters and prayers.

That is the key, she determined, to enriching your life with friends—"a little kindness, a little care, open eyes, and a little prayer."

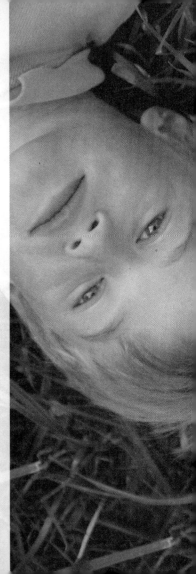

God, open my eyes so I may see
And feel Your presence close to me.
Give me strength for my stumbling feet
As I battle the crowd on life's busy street,
And widen the vision of my unseeing eyes
So in passing faces I'll recognize
Not just a stranger, unloved and unknown,
But a friend with a heart that is much like my own.
Give me perception to make me aware
That scattered profusely on life's thoroughfare
Are the best gifts of God that we daily pass by
As we look at the world with an unseeing eye.

God knows no strangers,
He loves us all,
The poor, the rich,
The great, the small.
He is a friend
Who is always there
To share our troubles
And lessen our care.
No one is a stranger
In God's sight,
For God is love
And in His light
May we, too, try
In our small way
To make new friends
From day to day.
So pass no stranger
With an unseeing eye,
For God may be sending
A new friend by.

I'm glad our paths crossed
    and I'm glad that we met,
And may this brief interlude
    prove to be, yet,
Something that helped
    to open the door
To the niche in life
    you were destined for.
For all that transpires,
    be it bitter or sweet,
Helps to make your life's pattern
    a bit more complete.
And sometime in the future
    may you look back and say
Our meeting was indeed a
    very lucky day.

Tried and True
Friends

Some friends became family to Helen early in life. She lost the men she loved most—her father and then her husband—by the time she was just 32. The good friends she'd had before became better ones. These friends rallied round Helen, and she found first solace and then, once again, joy.

"They know my moods, and love me anyway, have made me laugh and cried with me where there was nothing left to say," she told an interviewer in the 1950s.

Friends are the family forged in addition to the one you're born into, and they come to you at the most surprising times, in the most surprising ways. Once you have them, Helen advised a young friend, never let them go.

Friends are really wonderful
but special ones are few,
And they simply don't make them
more special than you.
For who but a wonderful friend
would be
As thoughtful and nice
as you've been to me. . . .
It's no wonder I welcome
an occasion like this
To send you best wishes
and a big hello kiss.
So consider yourself
most exuberantly kissed,
For you're one of the specials
on my friendship list.

You're like a ray of sunshine
  Or a star up in the sky,
  You add a special brightness
  Whenever you pass by.
  And all your lovely thoughts, dear,
  That make my heart rejoice
  Are spoken very clearly
  By your loving heart's still voice.
  For in this raucous, restless world
  We're small but God is great,
  And in His love, dear friend,
  Our hearts communicate.

Thank you for your friendship
  And your understanding of
  The folks who truly love you
  And the folks you truly love.

Almighty Friendship

Helen learned over and again in life that if not in presence, dear friends stay with you in memory. She'd loved so many people and lost so many friends to unexpected death. But as she was left later in life with fewer friends' presence and more of their memories only, a truth she'd long known became more clear— there is one Friend who never leaves. "I never really knew the wonder of Him," she confided to a friend in 1974. But she spent her remaining seven years searching the depths of this Friend, spending even more time with Him and singing His praises.

Apple blossoms bursting wide
　　now beautify the tree
And make a springtime picture
　　that is beautiful to see.
Oh, fragrant lovely blossoms,
　　you'll make a bright bouquet
If I but break your branches
　　from the apple tree today.
But if I break your branches
　　and make your beauty mine,
You'll bear no fruit in season
　　when severed from the vine.
For as the flowering branches
　　depend upon the tree
To nourish and fulfill them
　　till they reach futurity,
We too must be dependent
　　on our Father up above,
For we are but the branches
　　and He's the tree of love.

God is no stranger
    in a faraway place,
He's as close as the wind
    that blows 'cross my face.
It's true I can't see
    the wind as it blows
But I feel it around me
    and my heart surely knows
That God's mighty hand
    can be felt every minute
For there is nothing on earth
    that God isn't in it—
The sky and the stars,
    the waves and the sea,
The dew on the grass,
    the leaves on a tree
Are constant reminders
    of God and His nearness,
Proclaiming His presence
    with crystal-like clearness.
So how could I think
    God was far, far away
When I feel Him beside me
    every hour of the day?
And I've plenty of reasons
    to know God's my friend
And this is one friendship
    that time cannot end!

The unexpected kindness
    from an unexpected place,
A hand outstretched in friendship,
    a smile on someone's face,
A word of understanding
    spoken in an hour of trial
Are unexpected miracles
    that make life more worthwhile.
We do not know how it happened
    that in an hour of need
Somebody out of nowhere
    proved to be a friend indeed.
For God has many messengers
    we fail to recognize,
But He sends them when we need them
    for His ways are wondrous wise!
So keep looking for an angel
    and keep listening to hear,
For on life's busy crowded streets
    you will find God's presence near.

Now this book has ended,
You've read the pages through,
How grateful must be your friend
To have a friend like you!
For this gift from the giver was given
Wrapped with love and kindness and thought
In heartfelt appreciation
For the joy that your friendship has brought.

VIRGINIA J. RUEHLMANN

Whatever the celebration, whatever the day, whatever the event or occasion, Helen Steiner Rice possessed the ability to express the appropriate feeling for that particular moment. A happening became happier, a sentiment more sentimental, a memory more memorable because of her deep sensitivity and ability to put into understandable language the emotion being experienced. Her positive attitude, concern for others, and love of God are identifiable threads woven into her life, work, and even her death.

Just before her passing, she established the Helen Steiner Rice Foundation. Because of limited resources, the Foundation presently limits grants to qualified charitable programs in Lorain, Ohio, where she lived and worked most of her life. It's the Foundation's hope that in the future resources will be of sufficient size that broader geographical areas may be considered in the awarding of grants.

Because of her foresight, caring, and deep conviction of sharing, Helen Steiner Rice continues to touch a countless number of lives through Foundation grants and through her inspirational poetry.

Thank you for your help to keep Helen's dream alive and growing.

ANDREA E. CORNETT, ADMINISTRATOR
THE HELEN STEINER RICE FOUNDATION

One Final Page...

Jenna & Ashley
Best Friends